# Logic
# Puzzles

# BrainStrains™

## Clever
# Logic
# Puzzles

## Norman D. Willis

**Sterling Publishing Co., Inc.**
New York

**Library of Congress Cataloging-in-Publication Data**

Willis, Norman D.

Clever logic puzzles / Norman D. Willis.

  p.  cm.

ISBN 0-8069-8885-1

1. Logic puzzles. I. Titles.

GV1493 .W482  2001

793.7'4–dc21       2001049834

10  9  8  7  6  5  4  3  2  1

Published by Sterling Publishing Co., Inc.
387 Park Avenue South, New York, N.Y. 10016

This book is a compilation of excerpts from the following
Sterling titles:

*Mystifying Logic Puzzles* © 1998 by Norman D. Willis
*Tricky Logic Puzzles* © 1995 by Norman D. Willis
*Challenging False Logic Puzzles* © 1997 by Norman D. Willis

© 2002 Sterling Publishing Co., Inc.

Distributed in Canada by Sterling Publishing
<sup>c</sup>/o Canadian Manda Group, One Atlantic Avenue, Suite 105
Toronto, Ontario, Canada M6K 3E7

Distributed in Great Britain and Europe by Chris Lloyd at Orca
Book Services, Stanley House, Fleets Lane, Poole BH15 3AJ,
England

Distributed in Australia by Capricorn Link (Australia) Pty. Ltd.
P.O. Box 704, Windsor, NSW 2756 Australia

Sterling ISBN 0-8069-8885-1

*Logic puzzles require deductive reasoning based on given statements or propositions. The ones in this book will stretch your ability to successfully exercise reasoned trial and error and analyze alternatives. They may be challenging, but you will enjoy the satisfaction that comes from arriving at the correct solutions.*

# Dragons of Lidd and Wonk

*There are few dragons in the kingdom of Lidd, and they have been put on the endangered species list.*

*Dragons are of two types. Some have reasoned that devouring domestic animals and their owners is, in the long run, not healthy for dragons. They are known as rationals. Some dragons, on the other hand, are reluctant to give up their traditional ways, nor do they fear humans.*

They are known as predators. The king has decreed that rational dragons shall be protected. Knights caught slaying a rational dragon are dealt with severely.

In addition to being rationals or predators, dragons in Lidd are of two different colors related to their veracity. Gray rational dragons always tell the truth; red rationals always lie. Red predators always tell the truth; gray predators always lie.

There is something appealing to a dragon about being in a land in which knights are not constantly trying to build their reputations by slaying them. It was not surprising, therefore, that the blue dragons from the adjacent land of Wonk began appearing in the kingdom of Lidd. Blue dragons are rationals or predators, but they all lie.

To tell if a dragon is protected, it would help to know its color. However, there is an affliction endemic to humans in Lidd: they are color-blind. To them, all dragons look gray.

## One Dragon

A dragon is approached by a knight looking for adventure. The dragon, asked his color and type, responds as follows:

**Dragon:** I am either blue or gray.

What type is the dragon?

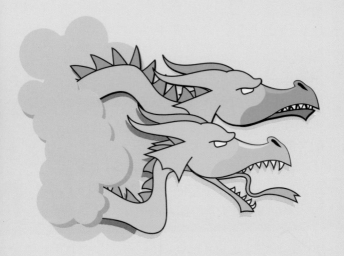

## Two Dragons

Two armed knights confront two dragons, each of whom is asked his color and type. Their answers follow:

**A.** 1. I am from Wonk.
2. B and I are both predators.
**B** 1. A is not from Wonk, but I am.
2. I am a rational.

What color and type is each dragon?

# Three Dragons

A knight in armor cautiously approaches three dragons who offer the following information:

**A.** 1. C is from Wonk.
   2. I am not a red predator.
**B.** 1. A is from Wonk.
   2. A and C are both rationals.
**C.** 1. B is from Wonk.
   2. B is a predator.

What is the color and type of each dragon?

## Two Are from Wonk

A knight confronts three dragons, exactly two of whom are known to be blue dragons from Wonk, and asks each his color and type. Their answers follow:

**A.** 1. B is from Wonk.
   2. I am a rational.
**B.** 1. C is from Wonk.
   2. I am a rational.
**C.** I am a rational.

What color and type is each dragon?

## One Dragon from Wonk

Three dragons, exactly one of whom is blue, provide the following information:

**A.** 1. C is a gray rational.
   2. I am a gray rational.
**B.** 1. A is a predator.
   2. A is blue.
   3. I am a rational.
**C.** 1. A is not gray.
   2. B is from Wonk.

What color and type is each dragon?

# Three Dragons Again

A lone knight nervously approaches three dragons, at least one of whom is from Wonk. They volunteer the following information:

**A.** 1. I am either red or gray.
    2. C and I are the same color.
**B.** 1. A is not red.
    2. C is blue.
**C.** 1. A's statements are false.
    2. B is not a rational.

What color and type is each dragon?

# How Many Are Protected?

A knight looking for a dragon to slay confronts three. He asks each about his color and type. Their answers follow:

**A.** 1. I am gray.
   2. We three are protected by the king's decree.
   3. C is red.
**B.** 1. I am not protected by the king's decree.
   2. C is gray.
**C.** 1. A and I are not the same type.
   2. A is red.
   3. B is a rational.

What color and type is each dragon?

## Who Speaks for Whom?

Three dragons respond to a very wary knight as follows:

**A.** 1. If asked, B would claim that C is a predator.
2. I am gray.
3. B is a rational.
**B.** 1. If asked, C would claim that A is a rational.
2. C is red.
**C.** 1. If asked, A would claim that B is red.
2. A is gray.

What color and type is each dragon?

# The Trials of Xanthius

*Among the ancient Greeks, the people of Athens led all others in their mental acuity. The gods created a series of trials to test the Athenians' reasoning ability, as well as their courage (and perhaps to amuse themselves). As an incentive, they provided a fabulous treasure to be won by whoever was successful in passing every trial.*

The trials involved following a path through a dense forest, across a large savanna, and up a tall mountain, with choices to be made at four points. There was to be no turning back once the challenge was accepted, and no retracing of steps at any time. Dire consequences awaited a challenger who made an incorrect judgment.

No citizen of Athens desired to accept the risk until Xanthius, a young student of Socrates, accepted the challenge.

## The First Trial

Hardly had Xanthius entered the forest on the designated path, when it branched into two. He was told that this was the first trial and that one way led to the second trial, while the other led near the domain of a giant serpent, for which he would undoubtedly become a meal. A sign at each path gave instruction.

However, Xanthius was informed that at least one of the signs was false. The signs read as follows:

**A**

> THIS PATH LEADS
> TO THE SERPENT.

**B**

> THE SIGN AT
> PATH A IS TRUE.

Which path is the one Xanthius should follow?

## The Second Trial

Xanthius chose the correct path and, after proceeding into the forest for some time, he came to a branching of the path into three paths. He was informed that one path led to the third trial, while the other two led deep into the forest and eventually into large circles, to which there was no end. Xanthius was told that of the signs at the three paths, two were true and one was false. The signs follow:

**A**

THE SIGN AT
PATH B IS TRUE.

**B**

PATH A IS NOT THE
ONE TO FOLLOW.

**C**

THIS IS THE PATH
TO FOLLOW.

Which path is the one to follow?

## The Third Trial

Again, Xanthius chose correctly and proceeded farther into the forest before the path branched into three more paths. His information this time was that one path led to the fourth trial. The other two led over large hidden pits that could not be avoided, and from which escape would be impossible. Xanthius was told that one of the signs at the three paths was false, and two were true. They read as follows:

**A**

PATH B IS THE
ONE TO FOLLOW.

**B**

PATH C IS THE ONE
TO FOLLOW, UNLESS
IT IS PATH A.

**C**

NEITHER A NOR B IS
THE CORRECT PATH.

Which path is the one to follow?

## The Fourth Trial

Xanthius, having made the correct judgment, followed the path until he came to a deep ravine over which were three bridges. He was told that only one of these could carry him over the ravine. The other two would crumble when he was halfway across, dropping him onto the jagged rocks far below. He was informed that two of the three signs at the three bridges were false, and one was true. The three signs follow:

**A**

C IS NOT THE BRIDGE TO CROSS UNLESS THIS BRIDGE IS NOT THE ONE TO CROSS.

**B**

THE SIGN AT BRIDGE A IS FALSE.

**C**

EITHER BRIDGE A OR BRIDGE B IS THE ONE TO CROSS.

Which is the correct bridge to cross?

# Problems from the Addled Arithmetician

*Letters and numbers—to the Addled Arithmetician they are much the same thing. At least it appears so, as he has them reversed.*

*In this section you will find addition, subtraction, and multiplication problems that he has prepared. Your challenge is to replace the letters with the correct digit. (A zero never appears as the left-most digit of a number.)*

As if mixing digits with letters was not confusing enough, the Addled Arithmetician has forgotten that each letter should represent the same digit wherever it occurs in a puzzle.

In these puzzles, each letter represents the same digit wherever it occurs in a given mathematical problem (above the line).

Wherever a letter appears in the answer to the problem (below the line), it represents a digit that is one more than or one less than the digit represented by the same letter above the line. For example, if B equals 4 above the line, all B's below the line will be equal to either 3 or 5.

## Addition, Six Digits

Each letter above the line represents a
digit that has a difference of one from
the digit represented by the same
letter below the line.

The digits are 0, 1, 2, 3, 4, and 5.

|   | A | F | C | E |
|---|---|---|---|---|
| + | A | D | D | B |
|   | B | F | B | F |

What digit or digits are represented
by each letter?

## Subtraction, Six Digits

Each letter above the line represents a digit that has a difference of one from the digit represented by the same letter below the line.

The digits are 0, 1, 2, 3, 4, and 5.

|   | F | B | A | C | B |
|---|---|---|---|---|---|
| − | D | A | F | E | B |
|   |   | C | F | D | E |

What digit or digits are represented
by each letter?

## Addition, Seven Digits

Each letter above the line in this puzzle represents a digit that has a difference of one from the digit represented by the same letter below the line.

The digits are 0, 1, 2, 3, 4, 5, and 6.

|   | D | G | A | E | C |
|---|---|---|---|---|---|
| + | E | F | B | A | C |
| C | F | G | D | G | F |

What digit or digits does each letter represent?

## Addition, Seven Digits Again

Each letter above the line represents a digit that has a difference of one from the digit represented by the same letter below the line.

The digits are: 0, 1, 2, 3, 4, 8, and 9.

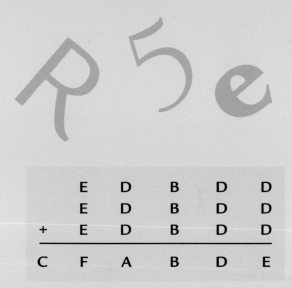

|   | E | D | B | D | D |
|---|---|---|---|---|---|
|   | E | D | B | D | D |
| + | E | D | B | D | D |
| C | F | A | B | D | E |

What digit or digits are represented by each letter?

## Multiplication, Six Digits

Each letter in the multiplication problem (above the top line) represents a digit that has a difference of one from the digit represented by the same letter in the answer to the problem (below the top line).

The digits are 0, 1, 2, 3, 4, and 5.

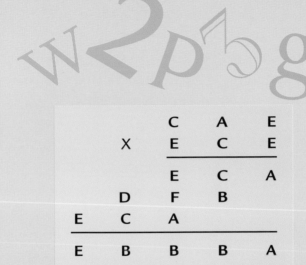

|   |   | C | A | E |
|---|---|---|---|---|
|   | X | E | C | E |
|   |   | E | C | A |
|   | D | F | B |   |
| E | C | A |   |   |
| E | B | B | B | A |

What digit or digits are represented by each letter?

## Subtraction, Seven Digits

Each letter above the line represents a digit that has a difference of one from the digit represented by the same letter below the line.

The digits are 0, 1, 2, 3, 4, 5, and 6.

| | | | | | | | |
|---|---|---|---|---|---|---|---|
| | B | D | C | A | B | F | B |
| – | E | E | B | G | E | A | E |
| | | G | E | E | F | C | F |

What digit or digits does each letter represent?

# The Land of Liars

In the Land of Liars the inhabitants are all liars, but not all the time. There are those who speak the truth in the morning and lie in the afternoon. The inhabitants in this group are known as Amtrus. There are also those who speak the truth in the afternoon and lie in the morning. The inhabitants in this group are known as Pemtrus.

Your challenge in each puzzle is to identify the Amtrus and the Pemtrus, and to determine if it is morning or afternoon.

## Two Inhabitants

Two inhabitants are known to be an Amtru, who speaks the truth only in the morning, and a Pemtru, who speaks the truth only in the afternoon. A makes the following statement:

**A.** B is the Amtru.

Is it morning or afternoon; which one is the Amtru and which one is the Pemtru?

## Two Inhabitants Again

Two inhabitants are asked the time of day. The two are known to be an Amtru, who speaks the truth only in the morning, and a Pemtru, who speaks the truth only in the afternoon. They respond as follows:

**A.** It is morning.
**B.** A is the Pemtru.

Is it morning or afternoon; which one is the Amtru and which one is the Pemtru?

# Two Inhabitants Once Again

This time, little is known as to the group or groups of the two individuals who make the statements that follow:

**A.** B and I are Amtrus.
**B.** A is a Pemtru.

Is it morning or afternoon; and what group or groups do the two speakers represent?

## Three Inhabitants

This time three inhabitants are approached. Two are known to be Amtrus, and one is known to be a Pemtru. They volunteer the following statements:

**A.** B is the Pemtru.
**B.** C is an Amtru.
**C.** A is the Pemtru.

Is it morning or afternoon; which two are the Amtrus and which one is the Pemtru?

# Three Inhabitants Again

Three inhabitants are asked the time of day. Two are Pemtrus and one is an Amtru. They respond as follows:

**A.** If asked, B would claim it is morning.
**B.** If asked, C would claim it is morning.
**C.** If asked, A would claim it is afternoon.

Is it morning or afternoon; which inhabitants belong to which groups?

# The Cases of Inspector Detweiler

*There are some within Inspector Detweiler's shire who do not always obey the laws. This extraordinary sleuth has been faced with several crimes that require solving. Your challenge is to determine which suspects are telling the truth and which are not, and who are the guilty.*

# Who Stole the Stradivarius?

A famous violinist was in town for a concert. While he was away from his room for a short time his favorite violin, a Stradivarius, was stolen. The inspector took immediate action and, through diligent research, was able to identify four suspects. Each of them makes one statement as follows. The guilty one's statement is false; the other statements are true.

**A.** I was not in town at the time of the theft.

**B.** C is the culprit.

**C.** B's statement is false.

**D.** C's statement is true.

Which one is guilty?

# The Forest Robber

A notorious robber has made a lucrative living by robbing travelers in the forest. Inspector Detweiler has, after extensive examination of the available clues, identified three suspects. Their statements follow. One makes two true statements; one makes one true and one false statement; one makes two false statements.

**A.** 1. I am not the robber.
    2. C is the robber.
**B.** 1. C is innocent.
    2. A is the robber.
**C.** 1. I am not the robber.
    2. B is innocent.

Which one is the robber?

# Nonsense

Here are two puzzles that may seem absurd and may not rely on any facts of which we have knowledge. There is logic in them, however, if you can assume that the statements are valid. Can you uncover the inference in each puzzle?

## Rabbits Play Hockey

1. Some alligators carry umbrellas in the shower.
2. Only those that know that flying fish live in the trees prefer caramel candy to chocolate.
3. Certain days are set aside for alligators to watch rabbits play hockey.
4. Some large reptiles are steeplechasers.
5. Only steeplechasers can watch hockey games.

6. Those alligators that carry umbrellas in the shower know that flying fish live in the trees.
7. Those that prefer chocolate to caramel candy cannot be steeplechasers.
8. Steeplechasers are vegetarians.

What inference can you draw from the above statements?

# Gorillas Enjoy Ballet

1. Gorillas are the only animals that enjoy ballet.
2. All animals can fly to Mars.
3. Scotch broom blooms every Thursday all over Mars.
4. Only those few animals that do not play solitaire are immune to hay fever.
5. No animal that travels in leaky rowboats ever has the penultimate word in a verbal discourse.
6. Scotch broom in bloom is what gives animals severe hay fever.

7. Those that do not handle hot ice cubes travel to town in leaky rowboats.
8. All animals that have the penultimate word in a verbal discourse play solitaire.
9. No animal that enjoys ballet handles hot ice cubes.

What can you infer from these statements?

# Answers

## Dragons of Lidd and Wonk

### Page 11

*One Dragon*

The dragon is a rational.

### Page 13

*Two Dragons*

A is a red rational. B is a gray predator.

## Page 14

### *Three Dragons*

A is a gray rational. B is a red rational.
C is a blue predator.

## Page 17

### *Two Are from Wonk*

A is a blue predator. B is a gray rational.
C is a blue predator.

## Page 18

### *One Dragon from Wonk*

A is a red rational. B is a blue predator.
C is a red predator.

## Page 21

### *Three Dragons Again*

A is a red predator. B is a blue rational.
C is a red rational.

## Page 22

### *How Many Are Protected?*

A is a blue predator. B is a red predator.
C is a gray predator.

## Page 25

### *Who Speaks for Whom?*

A is a blue predator. B is a red predator.
C is a red rational.

# The Trials of Xanthius

**Pages 30–31**

*The First Trial*

Path A is the one to follow.

**Pages 32–33**

*The Second Trial*

Path B is the correct choice.

**Pages 34–35**

*The Third Trial*

Path C is the one to follow.

## Pages 36–37

### The Fourth Trial

Bridge C is the one to cross.

# Problems from the Addled Arithmetician

## Page 42

### Addition, Six Digits

| A | B | C | D | E | F |
|---|---|---|---|---|---|
| 2 | 5 | 3 | 1 | 0 | 4 |
|   | 4 |   |   |   | 5 |

```
    2  4  3  0
 +  2  1  1  5
    4  5  4  5
```

## Pages 44–45

### *Subtraction, Six Digits*

| A | B | C | D | E | F |
|---|---|---|---|---|---|
| 5 | 0 | 4 | 2 | 1 | 3 |
|   |   | 5 | 3 | 0 | 2 |

|   | 3 | 0 | 5 | 4 | 0 |
|---|---|---|---|---|---|
| – | 2 | 5 | 3 | 1 | 0 |
|   |   | 5 | 2 | 3 | 0 |

## Page 47

### *Addition, Seven Digits*

| A | B | C | D | E | F | G |
|---|---|---|---|---|---|---|
| 2 | 3 | 0 | 6 | 4 | 1 | 5 |
|   |   | 1 | 5 |   | 0 | 6 |

|   | 6 | 5 | 2 | 4 | 0 |
|---|---|---|---|---|---|
| + | 4 | 1 | 3 | 2 | 0 |
| 1 | 0 | 6 | 5 | 6 | 0 |

**Pages 48–49**

*Addition, Seven Digits Again*

| A | B | C | D | E | F |
|---|---|---|---|---|---|
|   | 9 |   | 4 | 3 |   |
| 4 | 8 | 1 | 3 | 2 | 0 |

|   |   |   |   |   |   |
|---|---|---|---|---|---|
|   | 3 | 4 | 9 | 4 | 4 |
|   | 3 | 4 | 9 | 4 | 4 |
| + | 3 | 4 | 9 | 4 | 4 |
| 1 | 0 | 4 | 8 | 3 | 2 |

## Pages 50–51

### Multiplication, Six Digits

| A | B | C | D | E | F |
|---|---|---|---|---|---|
| 5 |   | 1 |   | 2 |   |
| 4 | 2 | 0 | 1 | 3 | 5 |

```
        1  5  2
     ×  2  1  2
        3  0  4
     1  5  2
  3  0  4
  3  2  2  2  4
```

# Page 52

## *Subtraction, Seven Digits*

| A | B | C | D | E | F | G |
|---|---|---|---|---|---|---|
| 0 | 6 | 3 | 1 | 5 | 2 | 4 |
|   |   | 2 |   | 6 | 1 | 5 |

|   | 6 | 1 | 3 | 0 | 6 | 2 | 6 |
|---|---|---|---|---|---|---|---|
| − | 5 | 5 | 6 | 4 | 5 | 0 | 5 |
|   |   | 5 | 6 | 6 | 1 | 2 | 1 |

# The Land of Liars

## Page 56

### *Two Inhabitants*

It is afternoon; A is the Pemtru;
B is the Amtru.

## Page 58

### *Two Inhabitants Again*

It is morning; A is an Amtru;
B is a Pemtru.

## Page 61

### *Two Inhabitants Once Again*

It is morning; A is a Pemtru;
B is an Amtru.

## Page 62

*Three Inhabitants*

It is morning; A is the Pemtru;
B and C are Amtrus.

## Page 65

*Three Inhabitants Again*

It is afternoon; A and C are Pemtrus;
B is an Amtru.

# The Cases of
# Inspector Detweiler

## Pages 68–69

*Who Stole the Stradivarius?*

B is the thief.

## Pages 70–71

### *The Forest Robber*

C is the robber.

# Nonsense

## Pages 74–75

### *Rabbits Play Hockey*

Only alligators that are vegetarians are allowed to watch rabbits play hockey.

## Pages 76–77

### *Gorillas Enjoy Ballet*

All animals can fly to Mars, but gorillas are among the few animals that should go there on Thursdays.